PO
KAPPA
MIKEY & ADDIE

by Robert Alan Evans

‖SAMUEL FRENCH‖

samuelfrench.co.uk

ISBN 978-0-573-12015-2

www.samuelfrench.co.uk

www.samuelfrench.com

FOR AMATEUR PRODUCTION ENQUIRIES

UNITED KINGDOM AND WORLD EXCLUDING NORTH AMERICA

plays@SamuelFrench-London.co.uk

020 7255 4302/01

Each title is subject to availability from Samuel French,

depending upon country of performance.

Author's Note

It's fun to look at your friends and decide what age they are inside. Some people I know are about five-years-old, still running around in circles, getting excited and hitting me on the head with rolled up bits of newspaper. Another person I know has the body of a forty-year-old, but is still about twelve inside; forever wandering around the playground looking at the tarmac and wondering who will be his friend. I also have a friend who is stuck at fifteen, listening to songs about misery and unable to throw away T-shirts that don't fit anymore. I think I am probably about ten. And that's what these plays are about. Being about ten.

Maybe being young really is easy for some people. I don't know. There were those ones who seemed to be good at everything. The ones who appeared to have a sophisticated grip on things that were, to me, a mystery; what clothes to wear, what music to listen to, who had snogged Bethan behind the bins. But I'm fairly sure that even they had moments of existential panic. When they were at home, staring at the ceiling, listening to the sounds of the house, surely they too wondered what it all meant and why things were the way they were. I, for one, had no idea, but one thing I knew for certain, was that it was not going to be easy and I would need all my wits about me, if I wasn't going to mess up and reveal the fact that I was completely and utterly confused.

When I was ten, I used to have the feeling that somehow I was being watched. We had bunk beds and I would sometimes lie in the bottom bunk and peel bits of woodchip from the wallpaper, then I would worry that the wall had people behind, just watching. They were scientists, I knew this because they had white coats on, were in a laboratory and some of them were wearing safety glasses (why they needed the glasses I never found out). And the wall would at some point lift up and reveal these people. They would confirm that my life so far had been an experiment. In some ways it would be a relief. Finally, it would all make sense. They would tell me that of course I was having these feelings, that actually everyone had them, that they had all just been pretending to see if they would still rise up in me. And they had, so the experiment was over. Everyone would be pleased with the results, pleased with me. What these feelings were, I'm not quite sure, as a boy who was gay they were probably about desire, but what matters is that I thought I was the only one having them. A play is a good way to ask questions, especially of a young audience, to ask why things are the way they are, to show that being young is not easy, to take their lives and their problems every bit as seriously as most theatre takes the lives of older people.

The plays are also a result of working with Andy Manley and Gill Robertson and as such are also filled with some of their experiences. They introduced me to working with young people and for that I will be forever grateful. To learn how to keep a young audience entertained is to learn precision, how not to be self-indulgent and the importance of being completely honest with your audience. They know when you're floundering around and they love it when you respect their imaginations and give them something difficult.

Finally, a note on all three plays. They are storytelling pieces. They can be told in whatever way you want. One actor, two, thirteen, it doesn't matter. In France, *Pondlife* has been told by a man and a saxophonist, a woman with a projector and once by fifty school children. They are written to be performed in theatres with full lights, sound and set and also stripped back to nothing, in school classrooms and halls, where a live performance can thrill every bit as much. This flexibility was always a goal of the work and an attempt to get good stories to young people wherever they might be.

Robert Alan Evans
2016

PONDLIFE

Created by Robert Alan Evans,
Andy Manley & Gill Robertson

Written by Robert Alan Evans

First performed by Catherine Wheels Theatre Company
on 2nd May 2008

This story begins with two men.

About my age.

Two men. Walking towards each other. That's the beginning and the end of this story.

And I'll tell you where.

An airport.

The lounge. Busy with people. Kids screaming, grannies sitting, mums perusing the perfume aisle, spraying clouds of Chanel No 5, already on their holiday. All waiting to board. Waiting to fly away to somewhere else.

No one notices these two men.

Except the cleaner. Mopping away. Sees them walking towards each other.

Two pairs of shoes. White patent leather come all the way from Los Angeles and brown brushed suede come all the way from Edinburgh.

Walking. Closing the gap.

About to meet.

For the first time in thirty years.

Best friends they were once.

Swore an oath on it when they were ten. Sitting in the woods one evening. Sky above going dark.

Best friends forever.

Didn't know they'd have a fight. Didn't realise their friendship would end.

But our story starts before then. Before all that. Back when they first met.

School bell rings.

*

Simon and Martin. Standing in front of P6 after the Easter holidays.

Martin looking around to see who he might make friends with. Shirt ironed, shoes polished, tie on straight.

And then Simon. Different. Long hair a mess over green eyes, his tie on wrong. Like it doesn't really belong to him.

The two of them standing, shuffling under the gaze of P6. Everyone already settled, already friends.

'Now Martin, tell us where you've moved from.' Mrs Nangle the class teacher.

'Now come on Martin, don't be shy.'

Martin knows this is dangerous. Hasn't had time to get rid of his accent.

'Birmingham.'

The class start to snigger.

'What did he say Miss?'

'Birmingham.'

'And does anyone know what you're called if you're from Birmingham?

No?

A Brummie, isn't that right Martin?'

Only someone who wasn't from Birmingham would say that, but Martin nods anyway, just wants to sit down.

Brummie. Brummie. It's racing round the class. Mrs Nangle saying something about spoons. About how Birmingham is famous for spoons and that makes everyone laugh more.

'Spoon face'

'Spoon boy'

'Class. Class. Now settle down. I don't want to hear any more remarks. Sharon MacGuinness and Colin Maxwell, that includes you.

Now, this is Simon.'

Simon nods. But doesn't say anything. The class stare, but he doesn't seem to care. He is staring at the poster of the solar system on the back wall. He just turns the collar of his jacket up and stands there. Waiting. Martin sees he has odd socks on. One brown, one green.

'Boys, you sit over there.' There are two spaces at the side of the class. Martin looks around, doesn't want to sit next to Simon, but there is nowhere else.

'Now class, as it's the first day back, I want you to draw your favourite day of the holidays. Let your imaginations run wild.

…

Not too wild Sharon.'

Martin gets up to borrow some colours. Maybe talk to some of the boys. But as soon as he approaches, each table seems to close up. No-one will let him near them. He goes back to his desk and there, in the middle, is the biggest pencil case Martin has ever seen. Old fashioned, like it's knitted, and overflowing with colours. Chalk pastels, oil pastels, huge fat felt-tips, everything you might need. Simon pushes them over.

'Thanks.'

'No problem', says Simon and gets back to his picture.

Martin gets to work drawing his pals playing football back in Birmingham. Then he notices Simon's picture. A blue sky with clouds drifting across the page, and something coming out of them. Soon it becomes a horse, a horse galloping out of the clouds. Strange but good. Really good.

'Hoh! That is amazing!' Judith Montgomery has come across, noticed Simon's picture.

'Miss! Look what Simon's done.'

The whole class stop.

'Simon McGurk! Well. Well. Well. It seems we have our very own Cézanne in the class.'

Everyone 'umms' and 'ahhs' at Simon's picture. Mrs Nangle sticks it up on the wall. Susan Topping says it's just like her horse Princess which she rides every weekend.

Only Sharon's voice can be heard complaining.

'It's meant to be your holidays. How's a flying horse your holidays?'

Breaktime.

Class pile out. Colin and Stewart barge past laughing. 'Out the way spoonface.'

Martin finally finds his way to the playground. A football's being kicked about. Thinks about joining in. In Birmingham he would've been straight in there. Right at the front. Calling to his friends. Shouting for the ball.

...

Leaves it.

Sees Simon on the other side of the playground. Alone as well.

Lunch. Martin stands with his tray looking for somewhere to sit. Just a sea of faces, then he hears a voice.

Sharon McGuinness, waving at him, smiling. Anoushka Osborne sits beside her, flicking her hair. And at the end of the table Colin and Stuart are playing Top Trumps.

'Martin!
Hey Martin!
Over here.'

'Martin. We were just trying to remember where it was you were from again.
Where was it?'

'Birmingham.'

'Where?'

'Birmingham.'

'Will you say something for me?'

'Okay.'

'Say "My name's Martin".'

'My name's Martin.'

'"And I'm a Bummy".'

'Shut up.'

'Bummy. Go on Martin. Say it.'

There's a crowd gathered now. All waiting.

'Say it!'

Stuart and Colin are watching now. Waiting for the fight.
Waiting for Sharon to turn mental.

'SAY IT!'

Wishes he was in Birmingham. Wishes he was back home.
Wishes someone would rescue him.

And then he hears a voice.

'Martin. Mrs Nangle wants to see you. In class.'

It's Simon.

'Says you've got to come now.'

Sharon closes in on Simon. Eyeballs him. He doesn't move.
She steps away. Away. Get away quick.

'What does she want? Mrs Nangle?'

'Nothing. Just looked like you needed a hand.'
And that was it.
They spend the rest of that day together. The rest of that week.

In class they start their project for the term.

'Prehistoric Man. The Stone Age.'

Mrs Nangle shows them a picture of a caveman. Neanderthals they were called.

Big hands drooping down to the floor. Jaw jutting out from thickset eyes.

Simon whispers that it looks a bit like Sharon McGuinness. Draws a picture of Sharon as a cave woman, hair wild, carrying a club and screaming.

Martin has to look at Mrs Nangle to stop from laughing.

It's so funny that they draw the whole of Sharon's table, all in a group, hitting each other with clubs.

Stuart, Colin, Anoushka and Sharon; The Neanderthals.

By the end of the week they have started to make a comic. Each story has the Neanderthals trying to do something, like inventing the wheel, but then they always end up hitting each other with it. Simon says that if he wants, Martin can stay over his on Friday and they can work on it properly.

*

Simon's house is one of the old ones on the hill. Martin's mum says they're drafty, but Martin likes it.

Simon's room is on the top floor and all the way up there are things everywhere. Enough to make Martin's mum have a fit. Books piled high, ornaments and pictures all over the walls.

On the landing is a deck chair with a parasol open, just standing there.

Simon's room is amazing. It's like a warehouse full of stuff; animal skulls, a dinosaur tooth, a glass tank full of stick insects. And stacked on shelves along a whole wall is Simon's pride and joy, his comic collection. All neatly sorted, he has everything, Batman, The Silver Surfer, the Fantastic Four. All going way back.

He tells Martin that if they do their comic right. Get it published. It could make them millions. Millions!

They get to eat pizza and work on the comic and later, as they go to sleep, they tell each other what they'd do with a million pounds.

Martin says he'd buy a plane and fly it round the world.

Simon says he'd buy the school and make Sharon clean it.

That term Martin's mum notices his room changing. New things appearing over the Aston Villa posters. A picture of a monster with the word 'Noush' written below. A crystal growing on some string and then finally, when she's hoovering under his bed, she knocks against something.

'What is this?'

'A sheepskull.'

'Where did you get it from?'

'Simon lent it to me.'

'It's disgusting. I won't have it in the house.'

'It's really old we reckon. Probably Neolithic.'

'What about other friends? Have you got any other friends?'

Martin shrugs.

'You should go out. Play football. You love football. Remember? Could never get you away from it back home.
Does the school have a team?'

'Don't know.'

'You should try out for the team. Get back into it. You were the best player back home.'

*

Martin doesn't try out.

Instead they work on the comic. Simon does most of the drawings and Martin realises he's pretty good at thinking up the stories. He thinks of one where Noush tries to eat Sharon and one where Stuart gets adopted by a diplodocus. At school they're pretty much left alone. And Martin's not bothered. He stops caring about football. Stops caring if people think they're weird. Together they're fine and the summer holidays get closer and closer. Then, in the last week of term, Judith Montgomery drops a bombshell.

'Sharon's heard about your comic. She reckons it's nasty. They all do. Says she's going to punish you. They all are. On the last day.'

Martin was terrified.

Five days to go till the end of term.

Five

Four

Three

Two

One

Martin wakes up. Thinks about Shazza's meaty hand hitting his face.

But Simon doesn't seem bothered. Just comes in and sits in class as normal. They put the finishing touches to the cavemen display and all the while the Neanderthals are looking over at Simon and Martin. Spooking them.

'Hi Martin.'

'Hi Martin.'

'You're going to get it Martin.'

Then, just before the final bell, Mrs Nangle notices something.

'Something's wrong with the display. One of the cavemen is missing. I think it's yours Judith.'

(aghast) 'Uhhhhh! Someone stole it Miss.'

'Now Judith I hardly think that's true.'

'It is. It is Miss. How else would it have gone?'

'Now class. I want whoever touched Judith Montgomery's caveman to hand it back. No harm done.'

But no one says anything.

'One last chance.'

Silence.

'Well, we shall all be staying here until someone speaks.'

'Oh Miss!'

Sharon McGuinness grabs her bag and slams it on the table in front of her. And that's when everyone sees what looks like a head roll out of the bag and across her table. Even Sharon just stares as it rolls to a halt. A pair of painted caveman's eyes looking back at her.

'No way Miss. It wisnae me!'

Martin looks at Simon and sees he is grinning.

'Right. Class. You're all dismissed. Have a lovely summer. Sharon McGuinness. You're staying right here.'

SONG: "MR BLUE SKY" – by ELO

Sprint out of school. Past the confused Neanderthals.

Past the huddle of kids.

No more school.

No more nothing.

Just SUMMER!

They crawled, and climbed, and reached, and grabbed, and hid, and whispered, and shouted!

They chased, and ran, and jumped, and caught, and laughed, and balanced, and fell.

Simon and Martin spent the whole summer together.

Smell of cut grass.

Mr Bridges walking his weird dog.

Radios playing the hit of the summer.

The gleam of it all.

An aeroplane scoping its way across the brilliant blue.

They ran. To where the town turned to country. They ran through the bit of woods.

They found a place where they could make a den. Surrounded by trees. Set a trap so if anyone came they'd know about it.

They broke and climbed. Climbed so you could see the hills, the town. Leaned back and watched the clouds.

They rolled down The Biggie. Headfirst sometimes. Climbed round the graveyard wall. Dead people, but they were alive. ALIVE!

Chopped the stinging nettles down with sticks.

Then the sticks turned into lightsaber as they finally saw the film everyone had been talking about.

Star Wars.

The noise of lightsabers.

'Help me Obi-Wan Kenobi, you're my only hope!'

'Use the Force Luke.'

They fight with lightsabers.

Then it came, the last day of the holidays. That evening they sit in their den and swear an oath. To stick together and never join the dark side. Never!

*

Thunder

First day back at school it rains.

Shoes wet. Summer gone.

They traipse into class.

Everyone the same, but different.

Colin's been to Spain and seen a bullfight.

Anoushka's been to France and seen a baguette.

Sharon's been to Bognor and seen a dead rat.

Martin sits next to Simon on a table for four.

The class stare at their new teacher.

'Right class.

My name is Truman.

T. R. U. M. A. N.

P7. Final year. You Will Be Adults. No more softy softy. Do as I say, when I say. Now. First thing. Wednesday. A trip. The Botanic Gardens. Hmmm. Exciting. You will take slips home. You will get permission. Second. Football trials. No excuses. You will try out. Understood.

So. Now. Art.

…

My Favourite Day of the Holiday.

…

Draw!'

Simon and Martin started to draw their summer. But Martin soon stopped and watched as Simon drew everything. Everything they'd done.

Mr Bridges' dog. The woods. The tombstones in the graveyard. But all mixed into one.

Mr Truman comes and stands behind. Looks at the picture.

'And this is?'

It's the holidays Sir.

'Mmmmm.

…

Ah! Now, Sharon isn't it? Much better. You can actually see what it is.'

'It's my sister Sir, in Bognor.'

'And in her hand?'

'That's the rat. She's the one that found it.'

*

Wednesday morning the bus comes to take them to the
Botanic Gardens.

Pile on.

Best seats. Where are the best seats?

Sharon MacGuinness barges past.

'Noush! Noush! Come on.'

Sharon and Anoushka claim the back of the bus. Sharon
showing off her new shoes.
Her new sparkling white shoes.
In front of them are the rest of the Neanderthals.
Simon and Martin sit halfway up opposite Judith Montgomery
who is telling everyone about her car sickness.

'My mum says I shouldn't sit over the wheel, it's worse when I
sit over the wheel. I've got special bangles. Magnetic bangles,
they stop you getting sick. That's what my mum said. Miss,
Miss! Do you like my bangles, they stop you getting sick?'

'Yes dear, very nice. Now P6 and P7 settle down, settle down.'

'SIT DOWN!'

'Thank you Mr Truman.
Right driver, off we go.'

The trip takes almost two hours.

It's meant to be fifty minutes, but they have to keep stopping to let Judith off the bus.

She's sick three times properly and twice just some dry retching.

Finally they get there and spend the morning in giant greenhouses like jungles.

It's amazing. Water dripping from the leaves and one giant plant that lets off a fart smell.

After lunch they get into pairs and have to fill in a quiz sheet.

It's a race round the gardens trying to find the answers. The colour of the bandstand, the name of the head gardener, the height of the tallest glasshouse.

Martin and Simon are doing well. Really well. With sticks as lightsabers they use Jedi mind tricks to get the answers.

The only thing they have left to do is find the pond and get the name of the boat there.

A sign for the pond points over a hill. They charge up it.

And there it is.

The pond.

And Sharon and Anoushka already at the edge, kneeling on the jetty.

What are they doing?

Then Martin sees that Sharon is untying the boat. Pushing it off so no one else can get the name.

Before he knows what he's doing Martin lets out a shout.

'Oi!'

And his lightsaber comes out of his hand. Did he throw it? He's not sure, but in mid-air it's suddenly just a stick. Coming down, arcing down. No. No.

It hits the water just in front of Sharon and splashes up on her. Up over her new shoes.

She looks up.

'You!'

And with that she's up. Up the hill and grabbing Martin.
No. Not Martin. It's Simon she grabs. And Martin doesn't
do anything. He doesn't say 'It was me'. Just stands mute as
Sharon pulls Simon down. Down to the pond.

Simon struggles.

'Leave me alone. Leave us alone.'

Gives a last look.

Then he's gone. Sharon has thrown him like a shot-put. Out
over the water. Right out and in. He splashes and the water
comes over his head.

Martin stands.

Watching as Simon comes up. Splashing. Panicking. He can't
swim. Knew that from the summer, Simon can't swim.

Why doesn't he do something? Why doesn't he move? Just
standing there.

Then...

Mr Truman rushes past.

He's down. Down to the jetty and in. In after Simon. Picks him
up.

The whole class are watching.

They all see Mr Truman trying to calm Simon who is thrashing.
Thrashing about.

'Shhhhh. Shhhhh. You're okay.'

Eventually Simon calms and that's when he realises he can
stand up.

The water only up to his waist.

He looks up. Choked and crying. The class are silent, just standing there looking at this boy, snot coming out his nose, exhausted. This thing covered in mud, weed, the wet green stink of the pond all over him.

And then Sharon says it.

'Look! Pondlife.

...

It's Pondlife.'

Everyone laughs.

'Pondlife McGurk.'

'Enough!' snaps Mrs Nangle.
'ENOUGH!
I want to hear nothing. You hear? Not another word.'

Pondlife.

Martin lends Simon his jumper.

He has to wear Mr Truman's shorts and a jacket from the driver.

He looks ridiculous.

But the worst is the squelching Simon makes as he walks back to the bus.

And the smell. Sitting on the hot bus. Rising off him. Everyone can smell it. Can see it. Wants to be as far away from Simon as possible. Whispers spread around the bus.

'Pondlife.'

'Pondlife McGurk.'

At home Martin thinks about telling his mum. Telling her how it was his fault. How he should've owned up.

Doesn't.

*

The next day at school everything looks normal.

Until they come through the gates.

The sound of 'Pondlife' being repeated around the playground.

In class no one will sit near them.

Even Judith Montgomery asks to sit somewhere else.

On the weekend they go to the den.

Try and light a fire, but everything is too wet from the rain. It just smokes and goes out.

Then finally Simon asks.

'That day, at the pond. Did I look stupid?'

'...'

'I'm sorry if I looked stupid. Just never learned to swim, that's all.

...

Just never learned.'

Martin wants to say, all the thoughts in his head. Say sorry for not helping. Sorry for just standing there. Watching. Simon must've noticed. Must've wondered why Martin didn't help. He doesn't know. Martin doesn't know why he just stood there. Why doesn't Simon say something? Why doesn't he ask? Just standing there. Just say something. Just ask.

But he doesn't.

'Should go home,' is all he says.

'See you tomorrow.'

'...Yeah.'

Monday and it just gets worse. Can't get away from it. Everywhere they go people pointing, staring. And Tuesday. And Wednesday. Pondlife and Bummy. Pondlife and his pal. Finally they are left standing on the edge of the playground. Trying to make themselves invisible so nobody will notice them.

And then on Thursday come the football trials. Have to kick a ball past Mr Truman and into goals. Colin and Stuart can't wait.

'Right boys. Colin!'

(*He saves the shot*) 'Ohhh! EASY!

Stuart!

(*He misses the shot*)

Lucky. I slipped there.

Simon...

(*He watches the shot go miles out*) Unlucky Simon. Maybe next year.'

Then it's Martin's go. He lines up. Takes off. Kicks a blinder. Like a bullet past Mr Truman and into the back of the net.

The others are impressed. Martin can see Stuart and Colin's mouths hanging open, surprised.

'Talent. Definitely. Mustn't waste it.'

Truman picks him for the team.

Stuart and Colin are picked too.

They stay behind for football practice.

'Right. First match. Longbridge Primary. You. Must. Win.'

They run, dribble, tackle, shoot. They pound up and down the field with Mr Truman, red faced, blowing on his whistle.

And Martin realises. No-one's calling him names. No-one's shouting at him. For the first time in ages he's lost in the middle of things. Not on the outside.

'Good boys. Good. You'll be a team yet.'

When they finish, Stuart and Colin say to him that they're going to carry on. Have a game later. Martin can join them if he wants. Get some more practice.

'Okay.'

At school Martin doesn't tell Simon about playing with Colin and Stuart. Just says it's a pity Simon isn't on the team too because he'll be practicing for the game against Longbridge. Simon says:

'That's okay. I'm getting on with the comic, I reckon it'll be finished soon. It just needs a final story from you Martin. Then we can send it off. See if it'll get published. Can you do one?

...

Martin?'

'Course. Course I can.'

Run, dribble, tackle, shoot. Martin practises every day with Colin and Stuart. Reckon they've got a good chance.

The day of the match. Pretty much the whole of P6 and 7 stay behind to watch.

The boys run onto the pitch. Get into position and they're off.

Not good.

Not a good start at all.

Longbridge get control of the ball.

Pass, work it up the field. Pass and score.

NO!

Then within ten minutes they've scored again.

NO!

By the second half Longbridge are walking all over them. The team is in disarray and Martin sees the whole of his class looking on. Disappointed.

And something changes.

Martin can feel it. Just…something takes over inside. Like he can see the whole of the pitch at once. Knows where every player is. He gets the ball. Runs with it. Fast. Dodging. Sliding. A defender runs towards him. He dummies a pass and sprints round. Another goes for the tackle, but Martin dodges and the defender slides across the ground. Finally there's nothing. Just him and the goalie. Feels the moment like it's solid in his hand. A frozen moment and he shoots. Scores. Yes. *(a roar)*

He scores not one, not two, but three goals and then it's the final whistle. Stuart and Colin pile him with joy. Lift him up. They're the winners. Martin's the winner. The winner.

The next day. Everything's different. People are still pointing at him, but Martin can hear what they're saying now. 'He's the one. Hat-trick Martin. Amazing!'

At lunch, standing in the canteen, Martin hears a voice again. Across the room.

'Martin!

Hey Martin.

Over here.'

It is Sharon waving.

Colin and Stuart are waving too.

Anoushka is looking weird.

Her head turned away.

MARTIN *looks around.*

'You.

Come here!

…

We saw you play last night.

Stuart says you were the best. Didn't you Stuart?

And Anoushka thought you were good too, didn't you Noush?

So, what you doing the weekend Martin?'

'Nothing.'

'You should come out with us. Might watch a film over Noush's.'

'I've got to go.'

'Where you going?'

'Meeting –

Meeting someone.'

'Pondlife?'

'…'

'What do you hang around with him for? He's so…weird. If you want you could hang out with us. I'm sure Noush wouldn't mind.'

'I've got to go.'

Simon's waiting for Martin by the field. Alone as usual.

'Thought you weren't going to come out.
Saw you talking to them. What were you talking about?'

'Nothing.
Football.'

'Thought you might be joining them. The Neanderthals.'

'...Yeah.'

Martin can see the others still sitting in the hall. Stuart and Colin having a laugh.

After that Martin stops spending lunch with Simon. Instead he stays in the canteen then joins the others playing football. He can hear Simon sometimes. Getting into trouble.
Pondlife.
But he's too busy running to notice.

They still sit together in class and sometimes go to the den after school. But more and more Martin hears his own excuses.

I've got to...
I would, but I've got to...
I can't tonight. I've got to...
Football. Homework. Even tidying his room becomes a reason not to be with Simon. Just the shape of him. Stood there. Looking at Martin. Like it's *his* fault he's called Pondlife. Like it's *his* fault that no one wants to be near him.

The one thing he does agree to is the comic.

'I'll finish the last story. I want to do it.

I've got an idea.'

And he did. He did have an idea. But for some reason every night he would unpack his bag and he meant to take it out, he meant to work on it, for Simon's sake, but he didn't. He just left it there. Underneath his football kit. Lying in the dark.

And every time Simon asks for it. He says the same thing.

'I'll do it tonight.'

Then one day. In the middle of a game Martin sees Simon coming across the playground. Something in his hand.

It's the comic. Crumpled and ripped now down the front.

'It was in your bag,' says Simon.

'You haven't done it, have you?

You haven't done anything.

I don't understand.

If you don't want to do it anymore. That's fine. Should've just told me. I would've done it myself. It's wrecked now.'

And Martin feels it. Something rising in him. This stupid shape just standing there, looking at him. Crappy old comic in his hand.

'So what?'

He grabs the comic from Simon's hand.

'You think this is important? You think our stupid drawings are important? They're not. They're crap. All of them.

I'm sick of them.

Look. Rubbish. *(he rips a page out)* Rubbish. *(he rips another)*

It's just kids' stuff.'

Other people have noticed now.

Martin and Pondlife. Arguing.

But Martin can't stop.

'You need to stop bugging me.

Stop hanging around.

I'm sick of it. Always there. Always looking at me.'

Colin and Stuart are there now, with the ball, and something about it. The ball. Martin picks it up.

'Get lost, Pondlife.'

It hits Simon on the arm. Bounces off.

He looks at Martin. Strange.

'What?'

Someone else has the ball now. They've kicked it at Simon. Hit him. He doesn't move.

Turns into a game. Hitting the ball off Simon who doesn't move. Just stands there. Until finally. Finally he can't stand it anymore.

'Leave me alone!

Stop it!'

Simon has tears in his eyes now.

He breaks. Runs.

And Martin turns too. Gets the ball and runs with it. Shoots. Scores.

But the goal's empty.

After break Simon doesn't sit with Martin. And Martin realises he doesn't care. He's glad. He goes and sits with Colin and Stuart. They make room for him. Welcoming him. He sees Simon sitting quietly alone. Reading something.

*

That year Martin became captain of the football team. Won the league too. His parents came and watched the final match and his dad punched the air when he scored the winning goal.

Simon had a picture published in the Evening Times. It was a cartoon of a lamppost peeing on a dog. He got paid 10 pounds for it.

They saw each other in the street sometimes. Walking to school.

In their final school photo Martin is between Stuart and Colin. Best pals.

Simon is at the back.

On the last day of school Mr Truman says, 'Do your best. Work hard. Make the school proud.' Everyone thinks, I will.

And that was it. End of primary.

That summer Martin spends most days with Colin and Stuart. They hang around town, play football. Then the other two are gone on holiday and Martin goes back to the den. Simon's not there. The place is the same. Still some broken bottles and burned out tins from where they had their fires. Someone else probably using it now.

Secondary school. Martin does okay.

'A bright and enthusiastic boy. Martin always gets on well with his classmates.'

Simon goes to a different school.

Martin thinks he sees him once. Going past on the bus. His hair longer now, but still Simon he thinks. Is it Simon?

And so time passes.

Martin grows up.

Gets a job

A house

Gets in his car every day and drives to work.

Forgets what it's like to climb a tree and see the world spread out below.

Forgets what it's like to score the winning goal.

Until one evening. His car stops at the lights and he notices something.

Just a cloud. Stares. And slowly he sees it. A tail. A body. The cloud becomes a horse. Galloping by.

And he remembers.

…

Simon McGurk.

Drawing in class that first day.

Long long ago.

His friend.

And the rest. It all comes tumbling in.

Playing round the graveyard.

Running through the woods.

Climbing.

Jumping.

Running.

Breaking.

And the beat of it all.

The sound of car horns.

And the lights have turned green.

Gets home.

Goes on his computer.

'Simon McGurk.'

Nothing.

Well, not nothing.

Ninety nine thousand results.

Then he thinks.

…

Might as well.

'Pondlife McGurk'

And it's there.

Top hit.

'Pondlife McGurk Animation.'

Martin watches a video of Simon. Suited now. Hair cut. Talking about the films he's made. People are listening. An audience. Come to see him. His old friend.

Wonders if Simon even remembers him.

Martin's never forgot.

That afternoon in the playground.

Throwing the ball at Simon.

Hitting him with it.

He never forgot that.

Thinks about writing an email.

Forget it.

He won't want to know.

Then he doesn't. He writes a letter.

"Dear Simon, it's funny, you won't remember me, but my name's Martin. We were friends once.

Wondered if you wanted to meet.

Probably not. That's okay.

Just wanted to say hello.

Yours, Martin… Neanderthal."

Feels funny that week.

Excited somehow. At work he notices, he's walking lighter.

Stupid. He won't write back.

Then a reply comes.

"Dear Martin,

Course I remember.

How are you?

Coming to London soon.

If you want to meet.

We could meet.

Best, Simon, A.K.A. Pondlife McGurk."

He goes to London.

Gets to the airport an hour too early.

Waits.

Watches everyone getting ready. Watches and waits. Waits for Simon.

And then it lands. The flight from LA.

Martin looks at his feet. Sees his brown suede shoes looking back at him. Wonders if Simon will even recognise him now. Older, fatter.

Looks up and sees him. This man walking down the concourse. Is it?

Is it?

And then the man looks up and Martin sees Simon in him. Sees his old friend.

Two men.

Walking towards each other.

Across a crowded airport.

One brown suede shoes.

The other white patent leather.

And I wonder.

I wonder what he'll think of me now.

Put out my hand.

Put out my hand to see if he'll take it.

The End

KAPPA

by Robert Alan Evans

NOTE ON THE PLAY

Kappa was originally performed directly in classrooms. The pupils didn't know anything was going to take place that day and their excitement at having a surprise story told over, under and around their everyday classroom space was truly thrilling. For the space of an hour Kappa is there with them and when he leaves it should feel that the story is continuing. It should feel that the seemingly normal world is full of secret stories, doorways and possibilities.

REHEARSAL NOTE

The play is written for one actor. For ease of reading, different characters lines are often finished with 'he said' or 'she said'. At the risk of stating the obvious it may be found that in rehearsals you don't need some or any of these, as the characters become more defined in the playing it will become clear to an audience who is speaking which lines.

Commissioned by Catherine Wheels and with Andy Manley, first performed in classrooms across Scotland in 2007

A classroom.

A man enters.

He has been through a rainstorm and is dry now, but his hair has that look like it is still plastered to his head, cut asymmetrically.

He is wearing a suit which has overtones of the future, a strange cut, though on closer inspection it may be a suit that has just been personalised.

He walks to the wall, examines it. He steps back. Looks at the class.

He runs at the wall and hits it full pelt.

He falls to the floor.

KAPPA 'scuse me.

He recovers and inspects the wall again. Tries to push his hand through it.

You haven't seen a door here have you?

There should be a door here.

Right here.

None of you have seen anything have you? Out of the corner of your eye? It might look like the air was shimmering. Like a patch cut out of the air. A doorway. No?

I don't understand.

I set the energy momentum tensor.

I worked out the cosmological constant.

There should be a door here...to a different world.

He gets out his tiny notebook and tries to work out equations. They are long and complicated. He notices the class looking at him.

What?

...

Why are you all here?

Someone replies school.

School?! This is a school?

Ha! Ha!!

How old are you?

Eleven.

I suppose... So...this is what you learn in?

My school was different to this. In my school there would've been a screen here with the teachings and each of us was plugged into it. We used to learn numbers; quantum, field theory, dimensional physics. I loved that. Could beat anyone at numbers. That was before the power started going. Ha! *(he finds something amusing in the classroom)* They couldn't afford to keep the schools running see. The power would go and school would end.

I'd go back home to Mum.

Mum?

My Mum.

She would say 'Wash your hands.'

'Don't spit'

'Tidy your room.'

'Do your homework'

Or, 'where've you been I was worried sick?'

Sometimes she'd find something so funny she'd laugh, like she'd have to leave the table from laughing and sometimes she laughed until she farted and then I'd laugh and she'd laugh some more.

I was eleven, like you, when I lost her.

Lost her?

...

That's funny, isn't it.

Gets out a photo of his mother. It has been ripped up and stuck back together with tape. It is very worn and there is a piece missing.

See. This is my mum. You can't see her that well because of the piece that's missing but she has brown hair, curly.

And brown eyes.

And she's got a mole just here.

You haven't seen her have you? I mean I don't suppose you've seen anyone like that?

Course not.

This isn't her world.

Going back to the photo.

She said we had to be a team because Dad was away. Working. She said it was just the two of us against the world.

We were a good team.

Until the day she stopped.

I suppose that's what started it all. That's why I'm here.

I was eleven like you when it happened. I remember that night.

Coming home from school and it's pitch black from the power cuts.

Not even a candle lit and I think Mum must've gone out, but there she is sitting in the dark in the kitchen. Smoking.

And I know something's wrong.

When she sees me she crumples up this piece of paper, but then she just looks at me and hands it over and she says 'I'm sorry'. Her last words. 'I'm sorry'.

And I look at the paper and it says my dad is 'deceased'. Deceased. My dad is dead.

So we sit there.

And I make Mum a cup of tea because she looks strange there in the dark and I light a candle between us, just to see each other, be a team, but Mum isn't really there. She's gone somewhere inside. And for the first time ever I feel alone.

Mum!

Mum?

Didn't know what to do.

Us sitting there. Had to do something.

So I cleaned. I tidied. I swept up every bit of dust in the room and still Mum sat there.

I emptied her ashtray. Made more tea. Nothing.

Every day kept busy.

Every day kept hoping.

For weeks I kept hoping.

Why didn't Mum say something?

Say something.

Please.

Please.

Don't leave me alone.

Mum.

I didn't know what to do. So I went to my room and lay down. I lay there and listened to the jingles.

FEELING BRIGHT AND BREEZY?
GET A SMILE THAT'S OH SO EASY.
MAKE YOUR MOUTH A PLACE PEOPLE WANT TO SEE
WITH TEETH SO WHITE DENTAL SURGERY.

And that's when it happened.

He makes a 'ping' sound.

The screen flashing in the corner. Covered in dust.

He finds a screen in the classroom and goes up close to read from it.

'Want to play?' it says.

Just like that.

Course everyone's connected to the screens. Got to be. Not allowed to turn them off. Don't even think they have off buttons. That's how you learn the jingles.

'Want to play?'

Want to play, question mark.

'How?'

'Plug in.'

So I do. The connectors are round the back and they're old. Boy, really old. Mark Sevens probably. Rusty too. But I get them in, and I feel the change, like you're slipping sideways out of your body and then... Oh! I'm in.

The web.

Far as the eye can see. Stretched out in front of me. All around, a look down and...

Eugh.

Right the way down, forever. *(He has vertigo)*

The web.

Haven't been on in ages. Not used to the feeling. Like you're floating, but there are things tugging you everywhere. Little pulls, like tiny hands asking you to come with them. The places that want you to visit them; casinos, clubs, the latest games, dream factories.

And I'm drifting, about to follow one when a voice is there in my head. Clear.

'Come on.'

'Where?'

'Follow me.'

I see a light moving off.

I follow. Right through the web. All the electric spots. Want to stop. Wouldn't mind some –

SUSHI®

COKA®

A ride on the new SUPERJET SPORTSTER™

A drift through MIRRORWORLD©™

But we pass by. Into the dark places where I've never been before.

And then here we are.
A sign blowing in the space wind.

'Old Papa's Game ShaK'

Like out of a ninja movie.

Go in.

We both sit round a table, a rock

And he says 'Want to play?'

He nods.

'So choose a name. Something you like. That's what you'll be called from now on.'

I look around. A name. On the table next to ours I see an ad for one of the old brands.

'Kappa. My name's Kappa.'

'Good. Kappa.'

'What's your name?'

But he doesn't tell me.

Instead, the game starts.

A tiny turtle appears. The logo from one of the old companies.

KAPPA *does a slow Tai Chi move.*

'Prepare yourself young ones.'

And that was it. We were off. Into numbers. That's what it was. A number game, but not your ordinary one, this was… I'd never seen it before. Intricate, like the cogs of an old machine. Numbers curling around. Spiralling and flying at one another.

7, 8, 18, 10

It was a quantum game.

So if you get the right numbers, work out the codes then tiny doorways open, into other realities, millions of them and you can pull things through the doorways. You can pull an apple from the air if you know the numbers.

And more than just apples. Unlock the right doorway and you can pull through almost anything. Three headed lizards, lightning bolts. We fired them at one another. Crackling across the universe.

And this guy was good. Better than I'd ever seen. He was sending things flying at me quicker than I could compute.

17, 27, 31, 46. Then he was into numbers that don't even exist yet. He started pulling them from the air. He was throwing the numbers at me. Smacking me about. Then one knocks me to the floor. And he's there over me, hand raised. *(He closes his eyes)*

He could've finished it, beaten me, but he doesn't...

'See you again Kappa', he says.

'Wait! What's your name?'

'Z'

And click, he's gone.

Back in my room and I don't even know how long I've been away. Could be hours, could be days. Mum! I shouldn't have left Mum.

Rushing downstairs.

'Mum!'

But she just takes a cigarette. Lights it.

In.

Out.

Doesn't even want to talk to me.
Doesn't even know I'm there.
Fine.

In front of the screen I sit and wait.

And wait.

And wait.

I wait until I've gone so far inside my body I can see my own eyeholes. Like I was looking out of my own face from way back. A tunnel to the world.

And then there's a noise.
Not on the screen.
Downstairs.

Just pushed under the door is an envelope.
He reads it.

'Kappa'

Inside is some kind of ticket.
'KING KONG 1 adult.'
And on the back, a message.

'Want to play for real?
Meet us.
Z.'

'Mum?

…

I'm going out.

He pretends she has answered.

I know you don't want me to. But we can't just sit here.

There's bread.

I'm going to take the picture of you. Just for luck.

Bye.'

He kisses her head and leaves the apartment.

Outside things were worse than they were before. Or maybe it just looked that way. The houses crumbling. Depression getting worse.

I stumble along. Where am I going? Don't recognise the place anymore.

Empty streets except for an old beggar sitting outside a shopfront.

Shouldn't've looked at him, but I do and he makes contact with me. He's only got one eye.

Then he's beckoning to me.

'Here. Come here. Down here. I've got something to tell you. I won't hurt. I just need to tell you something.'

So I kneel down. And he beckons me closer. *(gets closer)* Looks at me all sad like and then he gobs in my face.

Big phlegmy gob in my face and it's all over me. All over my eyes and I can't bear it.

And he's laughing. Can hear him laughing.

Cackles.

I run. Get away from the laughter. Get away. Get away. Get away!

I should've stayed at home. Should've stayed with Mum.

Run. I don't know these streets. Left right left right left. And then it's just me.

Lost.

And there in front of me. Across the street. The thing, the sign, the thing.

Big.

On top of a lonely building.

'KING KONG'

In GIANT letters.

And I see a movement up there. Behind the sign. A person. Slipping out of sight.

You know what I did?

I went up to the roof.

And that's where I met them.

The Gang.

Oh, you have never seen anything like these guys. Honestly.

Vicious.

That's how they looked.

But I was never scared of them, not even that first time. They were like me. Alone.

There was Deca. He's standing there, cool as a cucumber. Chewing on something. Gravel or something. You could see his blunt teeth like a row of pegs, all worn down. Smiling. Flicking his knife.

In

Out

In

Out

Staring at me. Like I was some kind of scum.

Then there's Siph. Pale. Like she's never seen the sun. Jet black eyes, and when she looks at you it's like she can see all your secrets. Can steal a wallet at fifty paces. I swear.

Move a little forward and see Epsilon. He's cool you know.
Big. Sort of guy you can trust. Maybe it's cos he can't speak.
Maybe that makes you more trustworthy.

I see the three of them and I know they're all waiting. I know
there's another. The one I've been playing.
From out of the dark comes this voice. From the shadow of a
giant 'K'.

'Want to play?'
And I feel something in me. Like a little voice inside me saying
'No'. 'Go home'. But then he comes out of the shadows...

And he looks exactly how I'd imagined.

'I'm Z,' he says.

'I'm Kappa.'

'I know. Look. King Kong. "K" "K"
I thought that would be suitable for you.
You like it?'

'Come on Z,' says Deca. Teeth grinding, folding his knife away.
'It's freezing. My headblocks are tammyshackled.'

'Fling your clacks,' says Z.
'I'm sorry. Deca's impatient. He wants to know if you're good
enough to join us. I told him you were, but he wants to see it
for himself. So what do you say Kappa? You want to join us?
You have to be pretty good with numbers.'

'I'm numbered up,' I say.

Deca snorts.

Then I see Z reach out and the next minute he's got an apple in his hand. Just like the game. But for real. Out of nowhere. He takes a bite. Then with a careful aim he throws it at me. It smacks into my head.

The others are laughing.

'How did you...?'

Whack! Another one hits me on the shoulder, falls to the floor.

'I told you Kappa, you've got to know your numbers.'

Suddenly he's firing more at me, apples, oranges, a whole set of screwdrivers – pulling them from the air. A snooker ball just misses my head.

'You can't. That's impossible.'

'Come on, flake him.'

'Deca here wants us to go. Thinks you're not worth it. Is that what you want Kappa? To be left alone again?'

'No.'

'Then do something about it. Come on.'

All the time throwing things at me. All the time having a go. The others laughing. Giving up on me.

'Come on Kappa.'
'Kappa.'

'Kappa.'

'Come on Kappa.'

'Is it Mummy you miss Kappa? Is that the problem?'

(eyes closed) I feel a flicker in me. Pure. Anger. I reach out.

And that's when it happened. The numbers in the air. I could see them and it was like I could control them. I open a doorway – a rip in the air – slip my hand through. On the other side I feel something wriggling, I grab hold of it and pull it back.

There in my hand is a rat, twitching in my grip. Wants to get out.

Z is smiling at me. Like I've done it. The others are smiling too. Impressed. Only Deca is looking like he might be less than pleased.

They're all waiting to see what I'll do. I run to the edge of the building and throw the rat. Far as I can. Skittering off into the night.

*

That first night we rack up in a hole. Wet underground hole next to the old railway. We light a fire and Z tells me the rules of the gang:

Live by night, sleep by day.

Keep moving.

And finally, 'Everything for the gang.' Keeping is stealing.

He said the world was rotten. Was slowly dying and how we were its kings now. How no one else mattered but us. Everything for the gang. He said that one day we'd leave them all behind. We'd find somewhere we could live, just us. We'd be a family.

Thought about going home then, it was late, but then Z starts telling more stories of other worlds and I don't know. I just forgot.

Wake up.

Siph is looking at me.

'You were singing,' she says.

'Was I?'

'You were singing one of the old songs. You shouldn't do that
…
Sing it again. Quiet like.'

'Which?'

'Shhhh, doesn't matter.'

She closes her eyes
I start singing, one of the old Coka songs

'YOU LIVE LIFE TO THE FULL
YOU NEED A DRINK THAT REFRESHES YOU
AND MUM AND DAD CAN DRINK IT TOO
IT'S A FAMILY DRINK THROUGH AND THROUGH.'

A tear comes down Siph's face then.
I go to brush it away.

'I'm fine,' she says.
'Just…haven't heard it for a long time.'

'Don't you watch the screens?'

'No. Z says they're poisonous.
He only uses them to find people. Like you.
…
He told us about your mum.'

'What?'

'How she left you.'

'She didn't leave me.'

'You miss her?'

'No.'

'I bet you do. I bet you miss her.

...

What's she like?'

'She's...' and I take out the photo and show her.

(**SIPH** *looks at the photo*) 'You should hide this. Just hide it away.

...

Now go to sleep. We've got a busy night ahead.'

She wasn't wrong.

That night we go to a late night t'ainment store. There's not much in it, mainly empty shelves, but at the back there's a whole rack of Red Devil. Z sets us up to get some, says my job is to grab the stuff, as many bottles as I can.

Deca walks up to Z.

'That's my job,' he says.

'Now it's Kappa's job. A chance to show us what he can do.'

Deca's not happy, looks like he might cry. *(in baby voice)* 'Oh poor Deca, is Deca not happy?'

Deca spits me a look that might kill a shark, but not me.

Edging my way through the store. Sweat on my forehead now, breaking out under my arms, cold sweat. See the Red Devil.

But the keeper's seen me too. Sweating away. He's watching me all beady eyed.

Can see Deca watching me. He's meant to be the diversion, but he just looks at me and smiles. Does nothing. Get to the shelf. Don't know what to do. What can I do with no diversion? Can see Z is looking at me. Tense. So I pull a bottle off the shelf look at it. Then drop it.

Does a smashing noise.

Explodes all over the floor.

The keeper stunned now. I pick up another bottle hold it up to him and drop it.

Another smash.

(several smashes) He's foggling towards me now. 'What are you doing? What are you doing? Stop!'

And then Epsilon – Yes! – Epsilon is collapsing by the mag rack. Pretending to have a fit. Ha! He's on the floor, wheezing and rolling around. The keeper stops, caught between the two of us. Siph pulls over a triangulation of cans.

And the whole store is in chaos.

I grab not just a bottle of Red Devil, not just a case, but the whole lot, into a trolley. I add to it a jar of mustard, some pickling onions and an entire barbeque set. Don't really know why I took that.

Then I'm running out past the keeper.

He's on the floor now.

'Stop! Please Stop! It's all I have. Please!'

...

But we are kings. We need it.

I run out.

We all do.

Out.

Out and away.

Finally stop.

Panting.

'You're crazy,' says Siph.

Crazy Boy.

'Am I?'

'Sure you are,' says Z.

'He didn't do it right,' says Deca. Angry at being wrong. Me having all the attention.

'He did fine.'

'What are we going to do with this? Mustard? Onions? You could've got us all skinned.'

'He didn't though, did he? No thanks to you.'

I think that gets Deca, Z saying that. Something switches in him.

'He's a faker. He's not even going to stay with us.

He's got a picture of his mum in his pocket. I saw him, and Siph all lovey dovey. I saw you.'

And then Z is looking at me.

'Is this true?'

'No.'

'It *is!* It *is!*', says Deca, frothing at the mouth now.

'Kappa?'

'You mean this? *(pulling out the photo)*
This is my mum.'

'You waiting to go home to her? Leave us behind. Is that it?'

'No.'
And they start to turn away. Give up on me.

'Hey Z. Watch!'

And I start to tear. I tear right through the middle. Down my mum's forehead, between her eyes. I think of her laughing, but I keep on tearing. Down through her nose and her lips. Right down the middle until she's two. Then four, then I keep ripping until she's in bits.

Z looks at me. I can tell he's pleased. I'm back again. Back with him.

*

Those first few weeks were a blur. I just have flashes now. Pictures of us. Dancing on rooftops as the sun comes up. Having a party in someone's abandoned swimming pool, howling at the moon way up there. We ran round town kicking up a storm. Soon everyone knew who we were, were afraid of us kids like we were animals. Feral. Got out of our way when we walked down the street. Whenever we could Z taught us the numbers. I was a quick learner. Soon I was beating Siph and Epsilon. Deca had stopped playing me, he was getting quieter and quieter as I pretty much became Z's number two. It began to feel like there was nothing else in the world but the gang. Really. Day. Night. It was all I could think of. It was like we

were in a boat on the ocean slipping further and further from
land. Towards... I didn't know.

Sings.

HAPPY BIRTHDAY TO YOU,
HAPPY BIRTHDAY TO YOU,
HAPPY BIRTHDAY DEAR...KAPPA,
HAPPY BIRTHDAY TO YOU.

Twelve, and Z's got a surprise for me.

Leads me into a basement where the others are sitting, all
except for Deca who's off somewhere moping.

On the wall is a sheet they've tied up.

Sit down.

Everyone's staring at this sheet and then the sheet is suddenly
white. Blinding after months of candle light.

And then it's there on the wall in black and white.

King Kong.

Haven't seen a film in years. Siph even has popcorn.

We watch as Kong is shot at, as he falls from the tower,
tumbling down and down and down.

I notice Deca's turned up. Talking to Z. He says he's got a
surprise too. Says it's a dare if I want it.

Course I want it.

So we head out.

And there's something about Deca I don't like.

Something makes me nervous, talking to Z like that.

What were they saying?

He leads us down streets and streets. A different part of town.

And I start to feel a familiar feeling. Like I've been here
before. Like a funny feeling inside. Like sick in my stomach.

And Deca takes us to a wall and says I just have to look over.

I don't want to. But Deca's not going to get me. So I do.

I look.

And there in a window is a woman, she looks old. But it's just because she's so thin, skin on bones. And she's sitting, just staring. And then she lifts her hand and I know who it is. She lifts her hand and tries to take a drag on her cigarette, but there's nothing there. Just an old butt. She tries to light it. Over and over trying to light this thing, but she can't. She's helpless.

Mum.

Feel the others looking at me. Deca sneering. And Z. I look at Z and I can tell he knew. He knew Deca was bringing me here. A test. Mum or the gang.

Fine. Come on then.

Jump down.

Come on. All of you.

Everyone looks blank.

Come on, let's go.

I run them through the dark.

See if they can keep up with me.

Z does. He's beside me running. Glowing in the dark.

Enjoying this.

And I think of Mum. Helpless. Don't want to think about her.

We run and run. Leave the others behind. Leave Mum behind.

Down streets left right left right. Don't know where I'm going. But I'm free running like that, the wind in my face.

And then I see him. The one eyed man. The beggar who spat in my face. He slips round the corner and I slip after him. Walk up and put my arm round him.

'Remember me,' I say.

'Remember!'

He's crying. He's scared of me. Doesn't recognise me.

I kick his legs out from under him. He's down on the floor now.

'Please mister. Leave me alone. Please.'

I kick him, soft like. And he's got his hands up to me now. Full of all his possessions. A watch strap, some bottle tops, an old coin.

Ha! I slap his hand and the bottle tops rain down.

And then I don't know what happened to me. I was going to leave him, just leave him, but his face there, looking at me. Helpless. Couldn't stand it. And so I did a bad thing. *(kicking)*

I did *(kick)*

a bad *(kick)*

thing. *(kick)*

Z has his hands on my shoulders.

'Come on,' he says.

'You've done it.'

That night we celebrate. I don't know what. My birthday, the things we've done. We dance. We dance until we're mad. And Z takes me aside. Tells me how we're going to leave. How we're done with this world now.

And I don't care. I don't care about anything. Just dancing. I dance and dance until everyone is asleep. And then I stop.

He sits heavily. Exhausted.

And I think I'm alone, but then I feel Siph's eyes on me.

'I don't think you should be here. You should go before it's too late.'

'Go where? This is me. There is nowhere else.'

'You still have somewhere Kappa.'

And then she puts something in my hand and wanders off.

There is my mum's photo. All stuck back together.

He closes his hand. Opens it. Looks at the photo.

I sat there until the sun came up, just a light in my eyes.

And I knew what I had to do.

I got up and I left.

Or I would've...

'Where you going?'
'I'm going home.'

'No you're not. You're one of us.'

'Please Z. Let me go.'

'If you're not with us then you're nowhere.'

And he pulls a knife from the air or from his pocket. Couldn't tell which.

And as I looked at him I could see there was flint in his eyes. I could see this was it.

He wanted me dead.

And I wasn't scared as he comes towards me I was just...tired. Wanted it to end.

But then I thought of my mum.

Thought of my mum and how I needed her. How she needed me. I couldn't give up. I couldn't. And at that moment I felt the numbers in the air. Felt them gathering round me. Look at Z. Knife raised.

I push the numbers. Further. Further than before. Until there's a rip in the air. A doorway big enough to go through. Into what though?

Z close now. Knife flashing

I step backwards through the doorway as I hear Z shouting

'Kappa!'

As I fall tumbling down and down and down. Into a new world.

*

And so that's what I do...

I travel. Through worlds. Looking for my mum. Trying to get back to her.

You haven't seen her, have you?

No, I already asked didn't I? Been looking so long I forget things.

And it's funny because when I do find her I don't know what she'll say. What will she say when she sees her little boy all grown up?

And the things I've done.

What will she say about that?

Will she even want to see me?

...

Well, I better go then.

Just...

He tries the wall again.

Must have the calculations wrong.

Goes to the door.

He doesn't want to go.

Oh. And if you see anything strange, you know in the way of doorways, shimmering air and that...you'll know what it is.

He's about to go.

Oh, and...thank you.

Exit.

The End

MIKEY & ADDIE

Created by Andy Manley and
Robert Alan Evans

Written by Robert Alan Evans

AUTHOR'S NOTE

The date on Mikey's birth certificate should be adjusted to make him around 10 years old at production.

Mikey is pronounced Mike-ee.

The show was originally performed by two actors. They split the lines, with one voicing Mikey's story and one Addie's, sometimes overlapping. However, this is flexible and left to the choice of the director.

First performed at the Imaginate Festival in May 2012, originally produced by macrobert and commissioned by the London 2012 Festival and (Scottish Government logo) supported through the Scottish Government's Edinburgh Festivals Expo Fund"

Okay.

So this will come together.

This story, like the universe comes together from lots of little bits. From seeing things. From connections. From the marks on the pavement. From a bag sitting caught in a tree. The first splodges of rain on concrete. From a bus trip to Glasgow and a trip back, silent. From all the millions of things that make up even one day on Earth.

Earth.

A cocophany of sounds. Radio waves. People. Traffic. Noise. Then up. Go up and just the sound of birds swooping. Clouds flying by. Up more. More. The thrum of ozone and then...

Ah.

Out.

There it is. Earth. Getting smaller below you.

Silent.

Spinning.

A little bubble of blue ocean and white cloud. A gem. Suspended in the black of space.

Then out further. Our sun.

Giant burning thing.

Imagine standing near to the sun.

If you could.

If you were fireproof. What would that be like?

Pull out once more.

Past Mars. A little more.

And there is a man.

Encased in a spacesuit.

We can't see his face.

Just the cut of the sun reflecting off his helmet.

Why would a man be here?

Floating off.

We could call out to him, but no sound would escape.

Space is a vacuum. We are all lost in it.

The man. Lost.

*

Then back. Back back back. Quicker quicker quicker.

Come on come on!

Flying back towards earth, the wind a sudden rush in

your ears as you fly in.

Towards land.

A continent.

A country.

A town.

A street.

A house.

A house.

Mikey's eyes

Addie's eyes

open at exactly the same time that morning. No one knows it.
Not even them. But they do.

*

Mikey sits up in bed.

Hits his head on Pluto.

It swings.

He stills it.

Looks down the line of planets that hang from his ceiling. Stretching towards the sun.

The sun, made from a mixture of bubblewrap and plaster of paris. He imagines it burning. A tiny ball of flame suspended in his room. That would be cool.

Around the planets are the stars; Polaris, Sirius, Alpha Centurai. Ninety five of them hanging from the ceiling. Silver foil catching the light.

And there, in the middle of it all hangs his dad, a small plastic astronaut.

Mikey touches his dad with a thought. 'I hope you're okay up there. God speed.' That's what people said at NASA and in books. God speed.

And with that he's up.

*

Addie has brushed her teeth, combed her hair and looked at herself in the mirror for eight seconds.

She had managed to ignore her little brothers for the whole of breakfast, which was a miracle really as they kept firing imaginary lasers at each other.

She had stared straight ahead and imagined they were dead.

It had worked.

Now she has laid out everything she needs for the day ahead. There are two baseball caps which she has personalised herself. They have 'Playground Monitor' written on the front and two ears, like fox's ears, stuck on the top. She doesn't really know why, but they look amazing and they'll certainly stand out in the playground. Then there are her handheld warning signs. Attached with elastic. One is red and says 'No' and the other green and says 'Yes'; they were to encourage good behaviour. And finally 'The Rules'. Her dad had let her print out thirty copies to stick around the school.

1. No running or dangerous behaviour (Addie would decide what was 'dangerous').

2. No littering.

3.   Climbing frame time will be managed by a rota. That way, everyone would get a turn.

4.   No throwing balls into girls' faces.

5.   No loitering.

It was perfect. She was going to be the best Playground Monitor ever.

*

Mikey walks through his kitchen with his mum's cup of tea. He likes to be so smooth that it doesn't even ripple.

He takes the step into the hall without raising the cup and walks along the hall like that. The hall half painted. One wall a kind of pink and the other bare plaster with patches of colour everywhere. His mum's testers. She had never decided which colour to do it.

The front room ahead. Boxes overflowing out of it. You couldn't actually get into the room. It was like the opposite of a room.

'The Box Heads'? No.

Up the stairs.

Careful. Careful.

His mum's door. Not a drop spilled.

'The Doors'? Already done.

His mum is sitting up in bed.

5, 4, 3, 2, 1.

Halfway to his mum he is weightless. Floating the tea in towards her.

She has to do the same. She nods her head slowly. Gives the thumbs up. He launches the tea towards her. She takes it and the spell is broken. Gravity back.

'Thank you Mikey.'

'Mission Control. Mission accomplished.'

'I washed your shirts. They're on the drier.'

'Yes ma'am.'

'And don't forget the money for the school trip. It's on the table.'

'Chhhhhh, message received Houston. Ending radio contact.'

*

They both leave their houses at exactly the same time.

Addie power-walks. She hardly notices the other groups of kids meandering their way to school. She wants to put up her rules before anyone gets in.

Mikey meets up with Stevie and the two of them walk in silence. Both of them trying to think of a name for their band.

'Blue,' says Stevie.

'No. Rubbish.'

'Tropical Delight.'

Mikey just laughs.

'Tropical Delight?'

'We could wear Hawaiian shirts.'

'Why?'

'Dunno. Just thought of it last night.'

'What about The Box Heads?'

'Squid-face!'

They pass by an old woman.

'Tartan Trolley?'

They had been doing this for weeks now, but nothing seemed right.

They were playing the school fair in two weeks and they didn't even have a band name.

Gordon joins them. Silently pulling up beside them. One foot on the pedal ready to hop off. He just rolls along next to them.

'All right?'

'Hey.'

'Anything?' asks Mikey.

'…Smorgen.
Just thought of it last night. It's all our names put together.
Stevie, Mikey and Gordon.'

Smorgen. Mikey waits to see what Stevie will think. Stevie
is silent. Waiting to see what Mikey will think. Mikey starts
nodding his head, slowly. He looks at Stevie who starts
nodding too. Soon they are all up about it.

'Yeah. Yeah. I like it.'

'It's okay, isn't it?'

'It is okay.'

'Yeah.'

'It's better than okay.
It's cool.
It's really cool.'

Smorgen.

Smor-gen.

SmorGen.

Now they just needed some songs to play.

*

Breaktime.

Addie rushes out into the playground. Her assistant Alison
trailing behind. Still trying to get one of her handheld
warning signs on.

'Come on! Come on!'

Alison had made them late. Alison was always making people
late. Addie had explained the new rules, had even acted out
a possible incident where someone had got wrapped in a
skipping rope and needed to be put in the recovery position,

but Alison had just stared at Addie through her big glasses. Fuzzy hair making her baseball cap go all wonky.

'Do you understand, Alison?'

'Yeah.'

'Really?'

'Think so.'

And then it was time. They had to get out there. This playground needed monitoring.

'You! You!' Addie shouts at a boy who is running too fast. She goes up and shows him her red warning sign.

'No running! It's dangerous. You might knock someone over.'

He stops and starts to walk. Addie feels a warm glow. It worked. She was really helping people.

Then she notices, behind the old shed, a knee sticking out. Then gone. What was it doing there, this knee? Someone was loitering.

'No!'

*

Sitting in the long grass behind the shed, Mikey has told Stevie and Gordon the first verse of the song he's been writing.

'It's amazing Mikey.'

'Really?'

'Yeah.
It's brilliant.
How did you think of it?'

'Dunno, just...'

"God Speed". I love it.
...
Is it about your dad?'

Mikey nods.

They didn't really talk about his dad any more.

When they were little they would talk about him all the time.

They had even turned Stevie's garage into a space station for a bit. They had slept in there in silver blankets that Stevie's dad had got at a marathon and in the night they had all laid their heads outside the door and Mikey had shown them the stars where his dad might be.

Now they never talked about it.

But sometimes, when Mikey was quiet, they knew he was thinking about him.

'Have you heard from him?'

'No.
He'll be too far away now. It would probably take years for a message to come back.
NASA will have stuff but…
That's what the song's about.
What it must be like to be up there. Alone. Trying to survive.'

The others all nodding. Thinking about it.

'Sometimes I imagine him, floating outside the ship, looking down at earth. Millions of miles away. We must be tiny.'

'What are you doing here?'

The boys scramble up. Hadn't seen this girl standing at the corner of the shed. Listening.

'It's dangerous. This whole area is off limits.'

'Says who?'

'Says me. I'm Playground Monitor.'

'So?'

'So! There is no loitering.
Haven't you seen the rules?'

The three of them shuffling.

And that's when Addie notices. Right where the boys had been sitting. A crumpled-up piece of paper. Her Rules.

'Who did this?'

No one. Not a sound.

'Who threw this away?'

'None of us.'

'They're stupid anyway,' says Stevie.
'Everyone thinks so.'

Addie caught for a minute. Did people really think they were stupid?

'They're making the playground safer.'

'They're making the playground boring. And why have you got ears on your hat?
You look like an idiot.'

'Well at least I'm not sitting here wasting my time talking rubbish.'

'We were having a band meeting.'

'Yeah right. You're not a band.
I heard you. Going on about spacemen and floating and looking down on earth.
You're like little kids.'

'You don't know what you're talking about.'

'You're just like my little brothers. Still making up stories. You're like babies.'

'We were talking about Mikey's dad. He's in NASA.'

'Stevie!'

'Your dad's in NASA?'

This girl suddenly on him. Her eyes boring into him.

'...Yeah.'

'Where abouts?'

Mikey shrugs. He can't look at her.

And then she's asking all these questions.

Going on and on.

Was his dad American?

You had to be American to be in NASA.

Was he a scientist?

What did he study?

Mikey doesn't know. He doesn't know what to answer. This girl going on about the NASA website now. How you can look up all the astronauts.

How they could do a project on him.

The whole school.

'...Well?'

'What?'

'Your dad. What's he like?'

'I don't know.'

'You don't know?'

And Mikey sees her face change. Looking at him differently.

'You're making it up.'

'I'm not.'

'You are.
Look. You're going red.
It's not true is it?'

'Shut up.'

'Why don't you know about him then?'

'Because it's top secret.'

'No it's not. It's because you're making it all up. You're talking rubbish. It's a lie!'

'I said shut up.'

And with that he pushes her.

She falls over. A sharp shock as she hits the ground. The others are all surprised.

Addie is surprised. She sits there a second. Then looks up at this boy. Startled. Why had he done that? They stare at each other.

And then he runs away. His two friends following. She looks down at her hand. Pulls it from a puddle, her warning sign bent over, the ink of the 'No!' starting to run. All of it starting to run as her eyes fill with tears.

*

Mikey sits in his room. Hunched up against the bottom bunk.

In his hands is an envelope.

Inside the envelope is a small plastic bag.

And inside that is dust.

From his dad.

It was moondust.

He'd got it in the post.

His mum had given it to him.

From his dad.

He remembered when he was six opening it up.

He'd only ever opened the plastic bag once and touched the dust with one finger.

It stuck to him.

A bit.

He didn't want to ruin it so he'd left it in the bag. Looked at it sometimes, but mainly he just knew it was there.

This moon dust.

His mum had given him.

Now he looked at it.

He felt stupid.

Suddenly.

He went hot with it.

This dust. Looked just like dust. Sand. Worn away rock.

The envelope. Had no marks on it. No American flag. No eagle and stars. It was just a plain envelope.

His mum had put something in a plain envelope and given it to him.

And then a postcard. From NASA. But nothing written on it.

Why hadn't he thought of it before?

He just never had.

Stupid.

…

His mum at the door.

'What are you looking at?'

'Nothing. Just a project. For school.'

*

Breaktime.

And everything is working well.

People are walking calmly and the climbing frame rota has been a success. Everyone waiting in line to use it.

In her hand Addie can feel her new warning sign. Smooth. She had laminated it this time. It wouldn't be getting wet again.

Then she sees him. Down by the back gate. That boy from yesterday.

Looking about. Opening it.

She goes to hold her warning sign up, shout 'No!'
But no sound escapes.

She just watches.

As he slips away.

*

Inside his house it's so quiet. Quieter than normal. Just being here this time of day. Not normal.

He runs up the stairs, two at a time.

Stands at his mum's door. Pushes it open.

He feels so wrong.

It all feels wrong.

Why is he even here? He doesn't know. He just has this feeling that there's something.

He goes to her drawers.

Nothing.

Just clothes. Jewellery. Her tights.

Nothing.

Looks about. The wardrobe.

Standing with the doors open he runs his hands over her clothes. A fur coat. The rough feel of sequins.

He puts his head in between the clothes and smells. Like he did when he was little. He can smell his mum. Opens his eyes and there. Below. A tin. Old. 'Quality Street'.

Of course.

He remembers it from when he was little.

He sits on the bottom of the wardrobe and opens the tin in his lap.

Inside are things to do with life. Things his mum has kept.

An old newspaper clipping from the 80s. 'Susan Harris raises one hundred and forty pounds through non-stop discothon'. His mum. She's funny. Alive. Only a bit older than him.

More things; a photo of his mum on holiday somewhere warm.

And there, underneath it all is a piece of paper. Small. Red edging. Important.

'Michael Bailey. 15th September 2006.'

His birth certificate.

He slowly reads across the columns; Mother 'Susan Bailey' Father 'Anthony Bailey.' Father's Occupation…not astronaut. Not even anything like it. Father's occupation, Plumber.

*

Addie sits at her desk.

She can't concentrate. It's annoying. She keeps staring out the window.

On a piece of paper she has written Life Plan and underlined it twice. She loves underlining. Underlining and hole-punching are probably two of her favourite things in the whole world. She looks at her life plan. Empty. Without taking her pen off the paper she draws a star. Then another one. Then she draws a line that goes all over the page and finally scribbles in big black letters 'Addie McAllister is an IDIOT'.

She scribbles it out.

Then rips the paper into tiny pieces.

Then scrumples it up and hides it in the bottom of the bin.

…

In the tree opposite her window she notices a blue plastic bag, caught in the branches.

Then she sees him walk past below.

That boy.

A connection. She feels it. Between the bag and this boy.

He looks empty too.

The wind blowing through him.

She creeps downstairs.

Why? She should be working.

And then she's out the front door.

What is she doing?

She's following him.

*

Addie doesn't normally go to the garages.

Other kids go there. Gangs of them.

Today though, she is here, and it's exciting.

Hiding behind the bottle bank she sees him lean against one of the metal roller doors.

He slides till he's sitting with his back against it.

Takes something out of his pocket. What is it? An envelope?

Something inside it.

He lets the envelope fall. Litter.

The thing left in his hands.

What is it?

He stares at it for ages.

Then lets his head fall back.

Hits the metal of the roller door.

Just gently.

He does it again.

The metal vibrates.

Then again.

Harder.

Until he's banging his head over and over.

The shock of it in the air.

He doesn't know what he's doing.

He's in a daze.

'You shouldn't do that!'

He stops. Still. Caught.

The two of them staring at each other.

'You'll hurt yourself.'

'So?'

'It's dangerous. Your brain will rattle around in your head and
swell up.
People don't know the dangerous things they do till it's too
late.
Like smoking.
If people could see the inside of their lungs they wouldn't do
it.'

'What are you talking about?'

She's not really sure.

'Are you following me?'

'...No.'

But it was too late. She'd left that pause. The liar's pause.

'I saw you yesterday. Leaving the playground. What were you
doing?'

'None of your business.'

'I should've reported you.'

'So report me. I don't care.
Just leave me alone.'

She can't even watch him walking off.

She's embarrassed.
Her.

Why is *she* embarrassed?

Why is she even here?

Then she notices something.

On the ground where he'd been sitting.

A little bag.

Dust or...something.

'Hey!' It was too late. He'd gone.

*

Outside his mum's room Mikey stands in the dark.

Can hear his mum breathing.

He wants to call out to her. Just say 'Mum'.

And she would tell him to come in.

Like she always did. Whenever he was scared or tired or just...

He would climb on her bed.

And she would stroke his hair.

His cheek.

Tell him the story of how she'd met his dad. The beach in Majorca. How she'd tripped over him, stargazing in the sand. How they'd fallen in love. Just like that.

He goes to knock on her door.

But he can't.

His hand just stays. Frozen there in the dark.

*

Addie lies in bed. On her desk is the little bag of dust.

It was amazing when you looked close.

All the little bits in it shone. Reflecting the light.

Now as she lies in the dark she can't help but think it glows. Just a little bit.

*

The glow from the computer lights up Mikey's face. The tap of the keys as he types it in.

Nothing.

Nothing.

Then there. Halfway down the second page.
'Anthony Bailey. Heating and Plumbing.'

*

Addie is late. She's slept in. Not like her at all. She'd been dreaming. Something strange. She tries to shake it off.

She brushes her teeth. Combs her hair and looks at herself in the mirror for four seconds.

Rushing out of the door her mum calls her back. Waving something. The money for the school trip. She'd forgotten it.

'Are you okay? Is everything okay?'

'It's fine. I'm fine.'

Out.

*

Mikey has packed his bag. A Mars bar, an apple, a pair of headphones, a t-shirt. That was the simplest. He looks at himself in the mirror. Tries to look older. A hat. That would do. Then out.

*

Two metres away Mikey walks out.

And then he's gone. Round the corner. Not the way to school.

What's she supposed to do?

Nothing. She's already nearly late. It's got nothing to do with her.

…

She follows him.

She sees him coming out of the cafe. With a T-shirt on.

Addie can't believe it. He's skiving off school.

'No!'

*

Run!

Chase.

At the bus station he searches.

Where is it? Where is it?

There!

He jumps on.

Goes to the back.

Sits.

Safe.

She didn't see him.

And then she's there. Scrambling on.

He can't believe it. What is she doing?

*

The driver staring at her.

What is she doing?

Asking if she's coming on or not.

And that's when it happens.

She gets out her trip money. Pays for a ticket. To Glasgow!

Everything.

Ruined.

*

When Mikey looks up she's there, sitting at the front. Idiot.

He puts his headphones on.

But he can't stop himself from checking on her.

And whenever he does it feels like she's closer.

…She *is* closer.

*

She's been tactically moving up the bus. Seat to seat. A teenager with a hat on. A man with an earpiece who keeps laughing into it. An old woman with a tiny dog in her bag.

She reaches Mikey.

'What?'

'You should be at school.'

He just looks at her.

Puts his headphones back on.

She sits down next to him.

The journey takes an hour.

Then they slow, come off the motorway. Stop at the lights. Mikey can see the buildings big now. All around.

Glasgow.

When the bus stops Addie doesn't know what to do, so she gets up.

As they get to the front a man stands up.

'Hey!

Hey! Aren't you Doctor McAlister's daughter?'

The two of them freeze.

'Addie, isn't it?'

Addie can't do anything. She just stares at him.

Then Mikey is pushing. Pushing Addie off the bus.

'Go.
Go!'

The man jumping off behind them.

'Hey!
Hey!'

But they are gone. They are lighting fast. The two bundling each other together through the crowds. Crowds and crowds of people.

Then Mikey shouts. 'In here.'

They dive into WH Smith.

It's like a film. Like the film where they get away from the baddies.

'Are you okay?'

'Fine. You?'

'Yeah.'

'Did he follow us?'

'No idea.'

They wait.

And wait.

Addie peruses the stationary aisle.

It calms her down looking at the staplers, rulers, the different kinds of pens.

And then there, right in front of her, a whole glass cabinet filled with dictaphones. Catching the light as they turn in the display.

She loves dictaphones. Her dad had one and sometimes he would let her record into it. Stupid things like her laughing or saying 'Hello'.

Her dad.

What was he going to say when he found out what she'd done?

She feels sick. Flushing hot and cold like that.

'We have to go back. Right now.'

'Go then.
I'll be fine.'

Inside Addie feels lost. This boy on some kind of mission.

She can see it.

Staring at an A to Z of Glasgow. Trying to memorise it.

A slip of paper in his hand.

An address scribbled on it.

'What's that?'

This girl. Would she never give up?

'My dad. I think.'

*

They have to get a bus. It crawls out of town. Way out to where the houses get further and further apart. The day hot now. Too hot.

The bus pulls away and they look across the road. A quiet estate. New-build. Each house with its own garage and green bit of lawn. Everything neat and tidy. They walk in. Round a curvey road and then there. Birch Drive. Same as on the piece of paper.

'Stay here.'

And she does. Stands still.

There was the house.

Mikey walks up to it.

'35' on the door in brass. All perfect. All obvious. Couldn't be clearer.

He pushes the bell.

Hears it ringing inside.

The last time he'd seen his dad it was the middle of the night. He'd woken up and caught his dad looking at him. Strange.

He had a coat on and Mikey had asked where he was going.

And his dad had looked around and picked up a star Mikey was making. Just a piece of silver foil. And he had stuck it to the ceiling and said, 'Here. I'm going here.'

And Mikey had believed him.

He'd replayed it so many times and now he wasn't even sure if it happened. If it had just been a dream.

He rings again.

Nothing.

No one there.

An empty house in an empty street on an empty afternoon.

He turns around.

Addie.

This girl.

She seems comfortable somehow.

He smiles to see her.

She smiles back.

He starts to walk towards her.

And then.

And then.

A car comes up the road behind her.

Slow like it's in an advert.

Silver.

It rises from the heat haze behind Addie. Like those adverts.

Gets closer.

A man and woman.

Mikey is halfway between the house and Addie. He stops. He's stuck on this car. Like a magnet. A force. Gravity.

He watches it pull up into the driveway. That driveway.

A second as it stops. Handbrake on. Then the doors open like they're in slow motion. This woman getting out. Tall. Blonde. She has boots on. Nicer than his mum's. She opens the back door and unbuckles a little boy. His hair blonde too. Curly. He is carried from his car seat and put onto his feet on the ground. Little. Two. Three. Mikey doesn't know. He wobbles a bit. Looks up at his mum.

She kneels. Takes the little boy's hand and walks round the car.

And a man has got out. Unclear at first, but now Mikey can see him. Opening the boot. He has a wax jacket on. The keys jangle in his hand. He pulls two bags of shopping out and closes the boot and that's when he turns. Sees Mikey staring at him. The two. This man. Connect. Mikey's whole heart stops. He cannot breathe. The whole world stops. This man. His dad.

From the house a voice. Her voice.

'Tony. Can you bring those bags in?'

'Yeah. Yeah.'

He turns back. Looks for the boy. Just standing there. But he's gone. Running away. He can see two of them. A girl and a boy. Running. He presses the key. A beep of the car. Walks towards the house. Slowly. At the door he looks back. That boy…

Then walks back and closes the door.

*

In the driveway outside her house Addie sees her dad's car.

Her dad.

Who is never home before seven o'clock.

Who says that work is the most important thing in the world.

Who must be home because of her.

She braces herself.

Goes in.

*

Mikey closes the front door.

Stands for a second.

He can hear his mum in the kitchen.

Upstairs in his room he looks at the stars hanging from the ceiling. Dead now. He finds the one that started it all off. He knows it. Has always known it. The most special star. He pulls it down. He holds it in his hand. He crushes it. And then it breaks. Something in him. He's pulling at them all. All the stupid bits of silver foil that he has hung up. The perfect. Most delicate universe. And he pulls it all down. Claws at it. Heaves and breathes and pulls until he's standing. Panting.

*

Addie's dad has told her off more than ever before by not saying a thing.

She came in and he just said 'Go to your room'.

He was so angry. She could see it.

'But' –

'Go to your room.'

Now she sits. Her certificate staring down at her. 'Awarded to Addie McAlister for Highest Achievement'. She can't even look at it. Why had she gone to Glasgow?

Outside a rumble of thunder. Way off. Something gathering.

*

Mikey's mum is at the door.

She looks shocked.

'Mikey?'

He looks daggers at her.

'What are you doing?'

'Leave me alone.'

'Mikey.'

'I said leave me alone.'

*

In the tree opposite Addie sees the plastic bag thrumming in the wind.

A flash of lighting. The world electric.

*

His mum.

Sees the devastation in his room.

'What is it? What happened?'

Looking at him like that. Like she cared.

*

Then all of a sudden the bag is attached by only one bit. She stares at it. Hypnotised.

*

'I know about Dad.
I saw him.'

*

One little bit.

*

He sees his mum crumble inside. Can't say anything. Just
looks at him.

*

She stares.

*

'All that stuff. NASA. Moondust.
You lied.'

*

This plastic bag.

*

'No.
Mikey.
It wasn't like that.

...'

*

Pah!

*

And then she tells him.

'You were just a little boy when he left. You were so sunny.
I didn't want to hurt that. You climbed on the bed and you
said that Dad had gone to space. You were so excited. I didn't
know what to say. So I said yes. It just stayed.'

*

Gone.

*

And that was it.

That was really it.

The truth.

*

Flying up and over the house opposite.

This bag.

Trying to tell her something.

What?

*

His mum staring at him.

Wanting to know. What would happen now?

He pushes past her. Burling down the stairs and out.

The first drops of rain starting to hammer the ground. Wet splodges on concrete.

A few seconds of stillness and then Mikey's mum runs out.

Pulling her jacket on.

The rain unleashed.

'Mikey!'

*

Outside. She hears someone calling. Loud. Desperate.

*

'Mikey!'

*

She looks out of the window.

Sees this woman there. Blown about in a mac.

And everything pours in. The whole day and the trip to Glasgow and watching Mikey as he came back towards her after seeing his dad.

That's why she'd gone. Because he needed her help.

She had to find him.

*

Sitting at the far end of the garages. Mikey sees the security light come on.

Then her shoes.

She sits next to him.

She sits.

Won't leave.

Won't leave.

Just sits.

Until he raises his head.

'I came to find you.

…

I'm sorry about your dad.'

And that's enough.

This girl next to him.

Mikey can't help it.

He cries.

He just cries.

And Addie does nothing.

She just sits.

Until eventually he stops crying.

'Sorry.'

'S'alright.'

'You must think I'm so stupid.'

'No.

…

…

Really. I don't think you're stupid.

...

I think you're quite good actually.'

'What?'

'Quite good.
Quite clever actually.'

He looks at her.

The beginnings of something.

A smile maybe.

Addie sees the streak of tears on Mikey's face.

She searches for a tissue. She always has tissues.

And then she feels something else. In her pocket.

She brings out the little bag of dust.

'What is it?'

'Moondust.'

'It's amazing. Have you looked at it? Really close? It's like it glows.'

He looks back.

'It does, doesn't it?'

And he sees her. This girl fascinated.

He takes the bag.

And does something he's never done.

He opens it and pours a tiny bit out. Into his hand.

Then he blows it.

So it goes everywhere.

A last flurry of wind taking it.

Sparkling through the air.

They watch.

Then he pours the whole lot out.

Spinning around. The dust flying up into the air.

Catching the light from the security lamp it shines.

And for a second the two of them see it in the air all around them. Next to the garages.

Their own universe of stars.

Suspended.

They look at each other.

Just the two of them.

Then up.

Go up.

A speck of dust rising through the night.

Mikey and Addie getting smaller below.

And we can see Mikey's mum and Addie's dad. Just reaching the garages.

And then up again.

They get smaller.

Smaller and smaller until they are gone, their town a sparkle of lights.

Then up further. A dusting of cloud now. Cold up here. Just the thrum of ozone. This speck of dust rising further. Faster and faster until we're out.

Out above the tiny planet spinning below.

Back and back. Past Mars.

And there is a man.

Encased in a spacesuit.

This particle of dust passing him by. A present from somewhere. Maybe a grain of sand from a beach in Majorca.

He watches the earth spinning far below. A cocophany of sound. Radio waves. People. Traffic. Noise. Life.

Lightning Source UK Ltd.
Milton Keynes UK
UKOW05f2136061216
289289UK00005B/189/P